Jane Doe
A True Story

authorHOUSE®

AuthorHouse™ UK Ltd.
500 Avebury Boulevard
Central Milton Keynes, MK9 2BE
www.authorhouse.co.uk
Phone: 08001974150

©2011 Jane Doe. All rights reserved.

No part of this book may be reproduced, stored in a retrieval system, or transmitted by any means without the written permission of the author.

First published by AuthorHouse 3/29/2011

ISBN: 978-1-4567-7492-9 (sc)
ISBN: 978-1-4567-7493-6

Cover by Stefan A Mack.

Any people depicted in stock imagery provided by Thinkstock are models, and such images are being used for illustrative purposes only. Certain stock imagery © Thinkstock.

This book is printed on acid-free paper.

Because of the dynamic nature of the Internet, any web addresses or links contained in this book may have changed since publication and may no longer be valid. The views expressed in this work are solely those of the author and do not necessarily reflect the views of the publisher, and the publisher hereby disclaims any responsibility for them.

A 4 year old once asked me:'why did the man walked into the fire'? I told her I didn'nt know, she said:' it was because he liked roasted nuts! It was the best joke I'd ever heard, not because it was the funniest but because even though she didn't understand it, she told it to everyone because it made her happy to see them laugh.

Don't dig the hole so deep
that you can't climb out of
it any more!

3 Years old

Mummy where are you?
Why am I in this place?
This is not my bed.
Why are all these tears in my face?

Mummy where are you?
Why am I all alone?
When are you coming to fetch me
From this children's home?

Mummy where are you?
Did I do something bad?
I'll be good now I promise.
I don't like it here I'm sad.

Mummy where are you?
I'm sure something is wrong.
Something must have happened
You wouldn't leave me here so long.

Sometimes the simplest things are the hardest to do!

I never got an explanation. To this day I don't really know why I was put into a children's home, and although I wouldn't wish the kind of memories I have, onto another human being. I have learned that a positive attitude takes you a long way in this life! So the life skills I learned from the experiences I had have given me the strength to achieve beyond anything I could have imagined for myself.

If you have had some past pain or disadvantages, turn these experiences to your advantage. If you can get through a traumatic time how easy is it then to do the simple things in life? All you need is a slight change of attitude. Find the positive side, there always is one, no matter how small, water it and it will grow.

Some of us were adults from the very beginning.
Some of us never got to be children!

4 Years old

PAIN PAIN
HURT BAD
HURT HURT
MAN BAD
SECRET SECRET
TELLING BAD
HURT HURT
MAN BAD
EYES CLOSED
KNEES WIDE
HURT BAD
MAN BAD
TELLING BAD
ME SAD

Turning your back doesn't really make it go away!

I have never exposed him! I could have! I googled him and found him! I have always suspected that I was not the first child he did this terrible thing to, and certainly not the last. "Host parents" come to take children from the homes for the weekend. These children get to be part of a "normal" family for these weekends. I guess it's a good idea for social skills to develop in underprivileged children.

It's just that not all these "host parents" have good intentions.

I went to these particular host parents pretty often, I remember them coming to fetch me for the weekend, I remember running to hide behind the building because I didn't want to go, I remember being found and kicking and screaming and crying that I didn't want to go to them for the weekend and being forced into the car anyway.

To this day I don't understand why none of the adults asked themselves why I so badly wanted to stay at the children's home on those weekends? Surely it must have occurred to one of the qualified staff, or perhaps the wife of that man that something must be wrong?

"A problem child" That's how they referred to me.

Adults, Please pay more attention to the children of this world. Sometimes there are good reasons for what seems to be bad behaviour. Children are so innocent and pure, we need to be there for them, and sometimes we need to understand the things they can't tell us.

Everything happens one day at a time.
Slow down and enjoy the good days!

5 Years old

Today I played in the sand.
Today my friend held my hand.
Today we climbed the big oak tree.
Today was a good day for me.

Yesterday a big boy put his thing down there.
Yesterday I cried but he didn't care
Yesterday two big girls beat me up with glee.
Yesterday was a bad day for me.

Never under estimate the effect a good deed can have on others!

A children's home is a tough place to grow up. You are on your own! No matter how old you are, you have to take care of yourself. Most of the homes are very badly understaffed, you pretty much raise yourself and your hygiene and health needs get taken care of.
When you are 5 years old that is not an easy situation to master, the older girls beat you up all the time. They too have a lot of anger to take out on someone smaller. The older boys were permanently cornering one of us, pulling our pants down and trying to do what older boys do. Life was just survival from one day to the next.

Every now and then someone would be kind. A stranger in a shopping store would say something nice or do something kind, a bigger kid would decide that today she would protect me. I held onto those kindnesses so tightly. They comforted me and gave me hope. They were the parents I never had.

If you have no children and you see a child anywhere, be kind to them. If you have children don't only be kind and patient with them, be kind and patient with all children.
The next time you see a child smile with all the love you have inside your heart. You just never know what is really going on in that child's life.

In the end the truth always come out!

6 Years old

I'm in school now
Where normal children go
But I'm from the children's home
I don't want them to know

An adult once said to me: 'If I could go back and know everything, I know now, I'd change everything!'

Of course it is embarrassing! It's a normal school. Normal kids. I wasn't normal. Kids are mean, they don't want to be, that's just the way it is. They tell it like it is.

I had to go to the dentist. I had seriously rotten teeth and the pain was getting rather bad.

Every Wednesday a half an hour before school ended there was an announcement over the intercom, "Would the children from _____ children's home that have to go to the dentist please come down to the office"

Now why in the world would I get up and go down to the office? Why would I want the entire class to know that I was in a children's home?

I had elaborate stories about my parents and my house and my pets.

Needless to say, once the toothache got bad enough everyone did find out that I was one of the children's home kids.

Most children don't like to be singled out unless they have done something good. Parents, teachers and adults take the time to be patient with children. "She is just a child and she must do what she is told." This is not an option. There is no such thing as "just a child."

I wonder where all these people are today? I wonder if they sit on there couches at night and feel proud of themselves?

7 Years old

The other kids have money and we have none
So the teachers touch us then they give us some
Break time, tuck shop, now we're all the same
No one knows our secrets
No one knows our shame

I could only wish that this book could land in one of there hands, or perhaps one of their daughters hands!

One of the not so great things about going to a normal school is the tuck shop. Normal children get pocket money for school lunch. We were so envious of this; we'd sit with our brown buttered bread in the freezing cold watching the other children buy warm soup or pies. Ever Friday there was a solution though; there were one or two teachers that knew exactly how to take advantage of this situation. They would keep us in the classroom for the first few minutes into break, please themselves sexually, and give us money for this.
The teacher part we hid somewhere deep inside ourselves, but going to buy that warm lunch was a really great feeling.

Children are resilient and adapt to so many life situations, even if they are evil and disgusting. If every adult reached out and helped just one child, imagine how many lives we could change.

It's such a terrible thing to hear,
the sound of a heart breaking!

8 Years old

Last night going to sleep
I heard other children's pain
Their little hearts sobbing
The tears falling like rain
Then I prayed to Jesus
To put there troubles on me
I was already damaged
Just let them be free

Imagine you see a dog get run over! You try to pick him up to take him to the vet, but he snaps at you because he is in so much pain. Would you leave him on the side of the road? No you wouldn't. You would find a way to help him...

I guess we always knew that even though we were the outcasts, we were not alone. We heard each others hearts breaking in the stillness of the night.

I will never forget the sobs of two particular little girls. They were sisters and there mother was in jail. I could feel their pain in the way that they were crying. It was so raw and so desperate, they sounded so broken.

I wished so much that I could take it away from them, it hurt to listen, I wanted to help. I just lay in my bed feeling for them.

I would imagine that those two little girls grew up to be tough and probably bitchy too. I would imagine that they probably have a small circle of friends and don't let people in easily. They may even be cold and hard, a defence mechanism they use to get by. Maybe you met them, maybe you didn't like them, maybe you gossiped about them.

Be nice to people even when they are not nice to you. I know that is not always easy to do, but remember those two adult women are still the little broken angels inside.

Of all that we see, or seem
Only half of it is true!

9 Years old

I'm a tough bugger now
I swear and I curse
Have you ever heard a sailor
Well I am much worse

You think you're a grown up
Don't tell me what to do
Fuck your maturity
I've been through mere than you

I may as well be 70 for all that I've lived
What you gonna teach me? You got nothing to give.
I stand up for myself, and all my friends as well
And if you don't like it
Fuck off and go to hell!

Life is made up of moments.
A good, fat laugh at something will make you forget everything, even if it's just for a moment!

At this age I was raw, I could only think and feel in extreme emotions. I had such rage inside of me I used to think that if I ran through a brick wall and watched all the bricks crashing to the ground, that I would be able to feel a little less angry. I didn't know where all the anger came from, I didn't think about it, it was just there. All I knew is that I had to protect myself from everything and everyone.

Children should not live lives where they feel that they have to protect themselves that is an adult's job. There is so much beauty and purity in children. They love to laugh and have the best sense of humour. They have the wildest imaginations and come up with the silliest ideas. We need to feed this, humour is the best medicine. Any child can show you that.

Children need an adult to talk to, they are not always able to understand there own feelings. The only way a child can grow up to be a normal, socially well adapted adult, is if they have one person in there childhood that loves them unconditionally. This person need not always be a parent, but the love must be unconditional. The inner strength and confidence a child gets from this is essential for his ultimate happiness.

If your mind was a plate of food, which meal would you be?

10 Years old

Swimming in a pool, blissfully unaware
A lady called me, she said somebody was there
It was quite a long walk, then a click in my head
I knew it was my mother, though nothing had been said

I couldn't remember her, not her smile nor her face
Not a look not a touch not a single embrace
There she was this stranger come to visit for a while
Making me so happy, this children's home child

Spaghetti Bolognaise?

Can you imagine for a moment what that must have been like. So many years of fighting for myself, so many years of abuse and violence and neglect. Then there she is, this person, your mother. It felt good because everyone could see that I had a mother and she came back for me, it made me feel more important than those children who's mothers didn't come back for them. But at the same time I felt uncomfortable, I knew I was expected to hug her, so I did. But she was a stranger to me. The situation was confusing and overwhelming.

Most children are afraid of new situations, they need explanations and preparation. What an adult may consider to be a great surprise is no necessarily perceived in the same way by a child.

Who ever said it was right! 'Let sleeping dogs lie!'

11 Years old

Holidays have come, I'm allowed to go to my mummy
Mummy mummy mummy mummy
" Hi that's right. I'm visiting my mummy"
I'm so excited! Holidays at my mummy.

There was lots of fighting
Between mum and new dad
Fist fights like in the movies
It made me very sad
The knife in the door
So afraid of what's next
Walked in the room
Saw them having sex

Back in the children's home
Don't say a thing
It was lovely with mummy
She pushed me in the swing
Don't say a word
She's all that I've got
Keep all her secrets
Or in the children's home you'll rot

Okay, so forget the Spaghetti, I'm thinking more along the lines of a Blender! Except the word smoothie is wrong, how about hacked fruit.

I had seen and experienced so many terrible things, so I wasn't really shocked. But I was very very scared. Their fights were so loud, so violent, they rumbled on the floor punching and biting and kicking. He locked himself in the bathroom, she was screaming at him repeatedly stabbing the knife through the door. I thought she was going to kill him. The worst part is, they fought like this almost every day. He was afraid of her, I was afraid of her, everyone was afraid of her.

And then she would sober up and be as sweet as an angel. Mostly she had little or no recollection of what she did when she was drunk, so I guess that in her mind she was innocent. She must have thought so because she never ever said sorry.

Don't build a life that fills you with regrets.
Build one that makes you proud!

12 Years old

Last holiday with mummy, after this I'm moving to her
I don't know what to feel. I'm confused I'm not sure
Maybe this time it will be different, maybe it will be good
Maybe this time it will be as a holiday should

My heart again is broken; she beat me black and blue
She says it's my fault for screaming Fuck You!
Well she dumped me in a children's home what did she expect?
That I'd grow up to be eloquent and courteous too?

Children's home or mum? Where do I live?
With mum is better, so I choose to forgive
I took all of my secrets and all of my fears
Then I opened my heart and she loaded me with hers!

Everyday is a new one. You get a fresh start every morning. Remember that and make the most of it!

I'll never forget that "punishment" In inverted commas because that was no normal way to punish a child. She beat me up very badly. That belt whipped around my body, my legs, my arms, my chest everywhere except my face. She was screaming at me and she beat me until she was exhausted. The biggest thing I lost that day was my pride. I begged her to stop, crying like a baby, I felt like such a coward afterward.
I was only a child but I never knew I could be a coward. I was black and blue for weeks after that.

Imagine looking into the face of a child, your child, someone else's child and being able to inflict such agony onto them. There is never a need to be violent with a child. If a young toddler that has put itself in a dangerous situation, like sticking it's finger into an electric plug, one could slap it's fingers hard as to ensure that he does not put himself into a situation like that again. Other than that I can see no good reason in the world to use violence as a form of punishment

Where one wall meets another
That's where I'll be
Curled up in a corner
No strength to be free

I can't find the reason
But I feel so alone
The winds of the past
Into my future have blown

The noose around my neck
Tightens ever day
No matter how I struggle
I can't get away

Time keeps passing
Days just fade
Freezing inside
Coz I live in the shade

It's my destiny
It's just fate
Happiness eludes me
It's a character trait

Born with the genes
Of tears in my eyes
Whish I had the choice
To choose another life

So where one wall meets another
That's where I'll be
Curled up in the corner
No strength to be free

I wish I could say that things turned out well, but unfortunately almost every day was like our first holiday. Can you imagine living your teenage years like that? Can you imagine watching the people that you love getting beaten up or urinated on? Can you imagine watching your mother spit into a coffee cup and then watching the guest drink it? And in the face of all this I had a terrible accident. I had multiple operations over a period of two years. I had to beg the doctor not to send me home on a Friday. The weekends were always filled with alcohol and violence. It was a nightmare. So many bad memories, so much pain and disappointment.

The most important thing is that you should never forget that you are special. Remind yourself of that every day! And even if you have not met the other people in the world that are suffering, remember that you are not alone. Be kind to yourself, be kind to others and most of all be kind to children. If you make a difference in one life, you have made a difference in the world!

The End

Lightning Source UK Ltd.
Milton Keynes UK
UKHW012301070223
416610UK00001B/239